Purpose

Life According to God's Plan

Florenza Denise Lee

Words to Ponder Publishing
Chagrin Falls, Ohio

For permission, contact Florenza Lee at contact@florenza.org
Words to Ponder Publishing Company, LLC
PO Box 1394, Hampton, VA 23661
www.wordstoponderpublishing.com and www.Florenza.org

Edited by Janice Allen: janiceallen7519@gmail.com
and Lissa Woodson: www.naleighnakai.com
Beta Reader by D. J. Mitchell: minibyme@aol.com
Cover Designed by J. L Woodson: www.woodsoncreativestudio.com
Interior Designed by Lissa Woodson: www.naleighnakai.com

♦ DEDICATION ♦

I dedicate this book to my family, Trefus, Jessica, and Missy, my most incredible supporters,

to NK Tribe Called Success for taking me under your wing and teaching this bird to soar; to my editors and beta readers for proofreading my work and giving priceless advice, corrections, and suggestions.

I also dedicate this project to you with gratitude for your support and prayer. It is my hope that through the pages of this book, you will discover God's purpose for your life and live authentically.

Purpose

Life According to God's Plan

Florenza Denise Lee

♦ ACKNOWLEDGEMENTS ♦

"Ye are the light of the world. A city that is set on an hill cannot be hid." (Matthew 5:14 KJV. First and foremost, I acknowledge that God is the center of my life. Through Him, I move, breathe, and have use of my being.

I wish to recognize Janice Allen, Stephanie M. Freeman, D. J. Mitchell, Anita Roseboro-Wade, Shawn Williams, J.L. Woodson, and Lissa Woodson. Most importantly, Naleighna Kai and NK TRIBE Called Success for the countless hours of mentorship, guidance, patience, and most importantly, friendship given to me as I transitioned from a Children's book author to adult literature

Florenza Denise Lee

Not all angels have wings. Some are adorned with scars like angelic symbols etched in runes of old. Her story started at the end. Tears like holy water nurtured the arid places in her soul better than blood. Forged in the flames of adversity, her scars became armor fashioned expressly for the battle ahead. There would be casualties; her innocence among them. The war raged on. And so did she.

Stephanie M. Freeman, author of *Necessary Evil* and *Nature of the Beast*

Author's Note

My journey begins with a vision I had of me walking with Jesus. As we talked, scattered hats caught my attention. Each had a single label attached to it. Looking at Jesus, He nodded approval. The word *author* labeled the *first hat*. Immediately, I plopped it on my head. The next one said, *daughter*. Yep, that's me. It went on top of the other. In total, seventeen hats were on my head: *author, daughter, mother, wife, sister, friend, prophet, evangelist, teacher, preacher, motivator, encourager, coach, advocate, radio talk show host, television host,* and *publisher*. Of course, I was delighted with the titles. After all, I hadn't even started my podcast, let alone thought of hosting a television show. Was this even possible?

With pride, I stood next to Jesus, desperately trying to show how appreciative I was of this remarkable gift.

He smiled.

Then it became too challenging to balance it all, "Lord, please help me carry this load."

Again, He just smiled and began to walk.

Struggling to maintain pace, I wobbled from side to side to keep everything upright.

When He stopped walking, I looked to find *another* hat—I wanted to cry. Yet something in His face made me investigate further.

Awkwardly, I ambled over then stooped down for a closer examination. Blinking, I could hardly believe my eyes. Was it as simple as that? Glancing back in complete shock, I saw Jesus smiling. Quickly, I threw all the hats I'd been attempting to maintain. With pride, I placed the single cap on my head. The word on it was— *obedience*.

What I learned through the vision was that no matter the titles we wear or the ministry we do, in the end, it comes down to obedience. Deuteronomy 28:1-2 reads,

"Now it shall be, if you diligently listen to and obey the voice of the LORD your God, being careful to do all of His commandments which I am commanding you today, the LORD your God will set you high above all the nations of the Earth. All these blessings will come upon you and overtake you if you pay attention to the voice of the LORD your God."

Obedience is a daily action. It requires we put away our desires and keep those of Christ foremost.

Luke shared the account of the anointing of Jesus's feet by an unnamed woman who worshipped him in the most untraditional way—she poured out on the feet of Jesus her life savings—all contained in an alabaster box.

There'd come a time in my life when I was lost. Not just figuratively, but literally. When God sent His angel most miraculously, I, like the woman, poured out all that I had in my worship and praise to Him. The following is my fictional account of her story. It doesn't replace scripture. It gives flesh to the unnamed woman in such a way that we connect with her *journey*.

What is within your alabaster box? Are you willing to lose it all for the sake of glorifying God?

"Be a lamp, or a lifeboat, or a ladder. Help
someone's soul heal. Walk out of your
house like a shepherd."

— Rumi

A Call for Help

Sixteen Years Old - 1980

"Suicide hotline, please hold."

If music played or if I stood there in silence, I cannot recall. What I do remember is my shaking hand cradling the receiver to my ear. The click of being placed on hold was the loudest sound I'd ever heard. I was in total disbelief. To this day, reflecting on that pivotal moment causes my skin to crawl. My vision blurred, then tunneled as my mind spun like a roulette wheel—around and round, it went. Holding my breath, I waited for the little white ball to stop. Secretly, I feared I was about to create a new landing space. If this proved to be accurate, I worried I would not survive.

The plush tan carpet found its way between blue-painted toes as my bare feet teetered on the edge of the first step on the landing. With sweaty palms, I gripped the handrail, fearing my knees might give way as I felt the cream-colored walls pressing in. Finding my voice, and it shook with fear. "Hello, is anyone there?"

Tears stung my eyes as I realized my lifeline had failed me. Yet again, I was left alone.

Fine. If I can't get help, I'll just do it.

It's surprising how determination manifests at the most inopportune time. Just moments prior, I'd lacked the strength to hold a phone to my ear. Yet now, I felt I could lift a car. I punched the disconnect button to end the call and stretched my five-foot three-inch frame as I reasoned within myself. *Perhaps they were counseling some other soul who needed assistance.* I prayed they'd at least received what I hadn't.

Phone in hand, I counted the eight steps back to the only bathroom in our three-bedroom home. Some might consider it a small house, but to us, it was a palace. Glancing to my right, I saw my brother's bedroom. He was the only boy and always had his own space. For a moment, I thought about tidying it for him but decided otherwise— no time to spare. I was on a mission.

The bedroom that I shared with my two sisters was just a few feet away. Bunkbeds flanked the far wall. A twin-size bed was parallel to it. Bed linen, curtains, throw rugs—nothing matched.

Without even looking underneath the single bed, I knew what was there, well-read books, and many. Each night, I read by the streetlight that flooded through the small window. If I had five cents for every time my mother caught me reading past bedtime, let's just say I'd have a lot of nickels. *I'm going to miss my books the most.*

I could not silence the woman's voice as it screamed, *please hold* inside my head, mocking my pain. What I interpreted from her actions was, "Who are you trying to fool? You aren't about to do anything irrational. Stop wasting my time."

"Oh, I'm not, am I? Then watch this." Stomping to the bathroom, I retrieved several bottles from the metal shelves and then lined the contents along the edge of the white porcelain sink. The thought to flush them down the toilet or wash them down the drain left as fast as it entered my mind. Overtaking me was a determination to be destructive.

When they find out I was serious, I bet they'll never place another caller on hold.

If the camel needed a straw to break its back, a call on hold was it.

"If you have a strong purpose in life, you don't have to be pushed. Your passion will drive you there."
— Roy T. Bennett, The Light in the Heart

Chapter One

Winemakers House: 33 A.D.

"For to us a Child shall be born, to us a Son shall be given; And the government shall be upon His shoulder, and His name shall be called Wonderful Counselor, Mighty God, Everlasting Father, Prince of Peace." Isaiah 9:6

Abigail's chestnut brown eyes stared at the wasp as it sought an exit by way of the partially opened window. Secretly, she wished she could sprout wings and fly away. She entertained changing places with the fly she'd seen earlier on the pile of dung near the cow pastures. The deep guttural moans and grunts snatched Abigail back to her reality, reminding her that she wasn't as carefree as the wasp. According to some, Abigail wasn't nearly as clean as the fly.

She knew this client well. He was one of her regulars. In just three more thrusts, he'd be done then on his way home to his wife and children.

Abigail tightly closed her eyes and gritted her teeth as wavy auburn hair plastered in perspiration to her forehead. Jacob wasn't a large man, far from it. He was of average height and weight, with kind eyes and deep-set dimples. His occupation as a fisherman had aged his skin significantly. His hands, rough to the touch, at times felt like grains of sand grating against her soft olive skin.

Out of habit, her right hand cupped the back of his neck and held his face close to hers. The scent of his sweat and the catch of the day transported her to faraway lands. What would life be had she been born a fish? Would she have traveled to lands unknown, or like his latest catch, been caught up inside a fisherman's net? With the way her life had panned out, most assuredly, she would've been someone's supper many times over.

Abigail opened her eyes and saw Jacob staring down at her. Had he been her husband, she might have enjoyed their interludes, but he belonged to someone else. Jacob was her last visitor of the day. Why he desired to visit after so many had gone before him was a mystery.

"My catch was good this week," he said over his shoulders as he bent down to fasten his sandals.

Repositioning to rest on her right elbow, she said, "That's wonderful news."

"It is indeed. Passover is approaching, and the additional income is much needed."

Abigail recalled the first time her grandfather taught her about the special holy day. She was eight years old. Lifting her petite frame high then placing her upon his lap, Abigail stared into his deep brown eyes, counting the lines as they stretched across his face—twelve. The number of the tribes. "The tenth plague on the Egyptians was when Pharoah agreed to let the people go."

The following year, she could nearly recite it. In her tiny voice, she said, "The Hebrews put the blood of the spotless lamb on their doorposts, and the Angel of the Lord passed over."

Beaming with pride, her papa nodded. "That's correct, my child. Elohim instructed Moses to warn the people to remain inside their homes. The angel passed over and did not harm those who were obedient. To those who weren't, and to all the Egyptians, the firstborn of animals and people died. Do you know why the plagues occurred?"

She startled when Jacob's foot hit the edge of the bed as he walked over to drop several coins on the bedside table. "I won't visit next week."

Blinking to focus, Abigail shrugged as though it was of no consequence. "If you come or not, you must pay my fees." She twisted her hair as she spoke.

"When have—" His brow furrowed, and he cleared his throat. Jacob sounded as if he might cry. "When have I not compensated you properly for your time?" His voice was barely audible. "Look, I've given you next week's fee and more."

She turned her face towards the window as Jacob touched her shoulder. His countenance fell as he slowly walked out the door.

Abigail pulled the sheer woven textile over her face and closed her eyes. She knew all too well why she'd become enslaved to the life she lived. Losing her parents at such a young age opened the door to abuses never told. Only when her grandfather came to redeem her did she find peace again. He went to his grave, never knowing all that her young body had endured.

Watching as the wasp escaped, she whispered, "The plagues came, Papa, because Pharaoh refused to let Elohim's people go to worship Him."

* * *

Her family owned a beautiful vineyard. Abigail's father, Aznar, created the best wine in all of Bethsaida. Customers called their home the House of the Winemakers. Families traveled from faraway lands to purchase the wine for their weddings and celebrations of births. Her parents died from leprosy before she was old enough to know them. Fearing the disease would spread to Abigail, her mother Diane begged Aznar to send their child to her grandfather, Malachiah. Unfortunately, it would take him three years to arrive.

As she grew older, Abigail learned how slow and painful their deaths had been. Leprosy affected the skin, nerves, and mucous membranes. The ulcers covered their entire body, from the top of their heads to the soles of their feet. Diane eventually went blind. Beyond the physical pain, learning how they were ostracized and left to live outside of town broke her heart.

She'd asked her grandfather, "Why didn't Adonai heal Momma and Daddy the way He delivered Job? Weren't they worthy of healing?" He reminded her that God's ways are not our ways, nor are His thoughts the same as ours. "We have to live by faith and trust that He has our lives in His hands."

"Papa, can I please see where they lived after they became ill?" She'd asked her grandfather when they moved from Bethsaida back to Jerusalem.

She'd only witnessed and endured tears in his eyes a few times.

That time he cried for an hour before finally saying, "I wouldn't want you to have that image seared in your mind, Abby. It isn't something a child should see." How she desperately wanted to share with him all the horrors she had witnessed, but like him, she believed that some things shouldn't be known.

Malachiah ensured she needed nothing. Abigail had servants who tended to her every need. Her caregivers had children her age, and they became the brothers and sisters she never had.

Tending to the fields was work but also a lot of fun. She'd play in the vineyard for hours on end, frequently returning home with a belly ache.

"Abby," her grandfather would call. "Don't eat too many grapes, or you may find yourself with a belly filled with gas." As he spoke the words, she emitted a gigantic burp.

"Better that end than the other."

Her grandfather had the best laugh she ever heard.

Malachiah once walked with her around the vineyard and smiled as he spoke. "Do you know why wine is so important to our people?"

Glancing through the straight rows of grapevines, she shook her head.

Her grandfather placed his wide but gentle hands on her shoulders as he turned her into a complete circle. "The prophet Amos said, 'Then they will live in their land. And I will bring the captivity of my people of Israel again.'" He pointed to her and then to himself. "And they shall build the waste cities, and inhabit them, and they shall plant vineyards, and drink the wine thereof; they shall also make gardens and eat the fruit of them."

He took a handful of grapes from the vine and ate them, giving her a small bunch to enjoy as they continued to walk. Malachiah gazed upon the crop. "And I will plant them upon their land, and they shall no more be pulled up out of their land which I have given them, saith the Lord thy God."

Wine-making was the only life Abigail knew until it was all taken away that she realized how remarkable her life had been.

Rising (with her mind inundated with thoughts of her current situation), Abigail pushed back the curtains as sunlight swept away the darkness of the life she lived during the night. Filling a basin with water, she washed her face as she peered into the mirror. Outside circumstances set her life in motion. Previously, she blamed everyone, then, only herself. She allowed fear to keep her in pain.

Abigail's home was well decorated. Yet, as much as she owned, peace was not one of the things she possessed. She felt as valued as the dirty foot-washing water in the basin at the door. Abigail couldn't recall the last time she smiled or someone touched her who didn't pay for it.

Chapter Two

The Market

Grabbing the pouch filled with ill-gotten coins, she exited through the massive archway. The walk allowed time for her to collect her thoughts and steady her nerves. Women with her reputation weren't always a welcomed sight.

The chatter from those purchasing their wares was louder than usual. Against Abigail's better judgment, she made her way closer to the crowds. She recognized the source of the excitement. Judith was flapping her arms like a wounded bird as she talked about something that had happened to her husband, Abe. His boss, Lucius, a Roman captain, favored him. Judith's full lips raced, causing lipstick to smear along her deep olive skin. Beautiful grey eyes sparkled as she shared the fantastic news with those listening.

Abigail recalled the first time she'd met Judith. She was talking to friends seated next to Abigail in the hairstylist tent. "My husband just returned from Capernaum." She twisted her head from side to side. "And this is what he brought me back." The gem-studded hair ornament was beautiful, the likes of which Abigail had never seen. It fit perfectly in her long luxurious tresses.

As Judith spoke to those who gathered around, the tone was gentler, kinder, not as braggadocios as when she showed the hair comb. "Abe was near death. He couldn't get out of bed, eat, or speak."

"Oh, no, Judith. We didn't know." Leah's hands covered her mouth as her eyes widened with disbelief.

Abigail was careful not to lean in too closely. But she wanted, no, needed to hear more.

"You aren't hearing me. I said Abe *was* almost dead." She raised her hands towards Heaven. "Praise Jehovah."

Shoppers stopped what they were doing and joined the ladies to hear more of the account.

"Lucius heard the Teacher was in Capernaum."

"You mean *the* Teacher who has been preaching in the wilderness?" Leah inquired. "I've heard when He teaches in the synagogue, He speaks with the authority of Jehovah."

Excited, Leah shouted out, "Did the townsmen told the Teacher how good Lucius was to them, and that…"

Loudly exhaling, Judith responded, "I was trying to get to that part."

Leah slumped her shoulders then lowered her head. "I'm sorry to interrupt."

"It is thrilling news. I understand your enthusiasm." Judith placed a gentle hand on her friend's shoulder. "They told the Teacher that Lucius had a beloved servant who was deathly sick."

A lady with doe-like eyes nodded with enthusiasm, causing her hair to cascade to the side of her cheek. Quickly repositioning the head covering, she asked, "So, what happened next?" Her voice squeaked like a mouse.

Abigail stepped closer, then quickly looked away, feigning interest in a pomegranate.

"When He spoke…." Judith's chest started to heave up and down. She placed both hands to her neck in a crisscross fashion.

Naomi rubbed Judith's back and consoled. "Take a deep breath. It's difficult to hear what you're…" She scrunched up her face, sniffed the air, then glared. "Is someone wearing nard? I despise that oil."

The ladies immediately looked at each other and then shrugged. The only women known to wear the fragrance were the town's harlots and the men who frequented their homes.

She locked eyes with Abigail. "You! What are you doing here?"

They caught Naomi by her arm, restraining her from moving closer.

"You should be stoned, you harlot." Rage filled her eyes, and spittle landed on her chin.

Abigail didn't flinch. She'd learned how to handle angry wives a long time ago. Harlots weren't the problem. Unfaithful men were.

Abigail was the one who should be angry—at the entire world. She was just fourteen when for the second time, her life turned upside down. Her grandfather had granted her permission to go and stay with friends from her hometown. She was so very homesick and needed to be near where her parents' memory was strongest.

Although it occurred years ago, the memory was as vivid to Abigail as if it were yesterday.

"Abigail," Ruth whispered. "I heard my father mention healing occurs at the pool in Bethesda."

"Do you believe him?" She rubbed her left hand with her right thumb.

"I know that he wouldn't lie. He told my mother God sent an angel to stir the waters. The first person in is healed."

Abigail allowed this to settle in her mind. "What if someone reaches the water first and is healed before I could get in?"

"That's a possibility. However, if we don't try, you'll never know." From the day Abigail confided in her what had happened, she desperately wanted her cousin to be healed from her broken heart.

Roughly an hour passed as they contemplated how they'd make the voyage. Ruth was sure they could make the journey; her dad's workers could ensure their safe arrival and vouch for their whereabouts.

"Let's do it." Abigail cheered.

"Do what?" The six-foot frame of Ruth's dad, Caleb, blocked the light as he stood in the doorway. His eyes lacked the usual twinkle Abigail had come to love. Two years following her parent's death, Caleb and Anna were like parents in their absence.

"Hi, Dad." Ruth ran over to him. "We were just planning our next adventure." She winked at Abigail.

"I have sad news." He came and sat on the bed. "I'm afraid there has been some news regarding Malachiah."

Both girls gasped in unison.

"Is my grandfather doing well?" Tears stung Abigail's eyes before the words left her mouth.

Ruth immediately intertwined her arm into hers.

"We'll find out more when we get you home." Looking at the packed bags near the bed, he reached for Abigail's things and asked, "What sort of trouble were you two about to get into?"

"Nothing that matters now," Abigail said, sadness filling her heart. "Nothing at all."

*"Your purpose in life is to find your purpose
and give your whole heart and soul to it."*
                                    — Buddha

Chapter Three

The Truth

Shaking the painful memory from her mind, Abigail walked towards the far side of the market. As she enjoyed the last bite of the delicious red fruit, a gust of wind carried the sweet aromas from the oils and fragrances shop.

"Are you certain this is the box you want?" Deborah had asked that day Abigail when first she came to the shop.

Abigail bent over for a closer look. It wasn't like the one her grandfather had given her, but it was just as beautiful.

"It's called—"

"An alabastron," Abigail said. "I had one as a child."

Deborah reached for a white woven cloth to cover her hands before picking it up. "This one is perfect for storing perfumes and oils."

Abigail swatted away a fly that had landed on her arm. "My grandfather told me of boxes made from gold, glass, clay, woven threads, silver, and ivory. He said they originate from Egypt."

Deborah clasped her hands, "Your grandfather would've been a great assistant. Alabaster boxes are for dowries and burials."

Abigail visually traced the intricate engravings.

"King Solomon's temple had the same stone," Deborah said proudly.

Silently, her lips moved as she recalled the grandfather quoting a verse in the Song of Songs.

"When filled, I seal the box with wax to prevent the perfume from escaping," Deborah said.

Abigail walked around the shop looking at other items. She eventually returned to the object that had first captured her attention. "Will it keep for a very long time?"

"It'll last for an eternity. Would you like to hold it?" She set the box down and pulled another cloth from the pocket of her tunic.

It was weightier than she expected. "How much oil will it contain?"

Scratching the thinning grey hair under her covering, Deborah responded, "Approximately three hundred days' wages worth."

"I'd like this one."

Deborah wrapped it in the cloth and extended it to Abigail as she placed the coins in the pocket of her robe.

"If you don't mind, may I leave it here?" Abigail asked, stepping to the right as if avoiding questions. "I'll return periodically to purchase oils to add to it."

There was sadness in Deborah's eyes. The woman's husband had passed away years before. Had it not been for their business, she and her young sons would've been beggars in the streets. Now those grown men had families of their own.

"I can always use help here. Why not come to work for me?" Deborah offered.

Abigail politely refused the offer, adding, "I appreciate your kindness."

* * *

"Abigail?" Although many years had passed since they'd first met, Deborah still lovingly greeted her when she visited the shop. "How're you today, my child? I didn't expect to see you again so soon."

Wiping the pomegranate juice from her fingers on her skirt, Abigail returned the embrace wholeheartedly.

Deborah pointed to a seat covered with several pillows. "I have a new fragrance I was just about to inspect." She walked over to remove a blue bottle from a shelf. "May I?'"

Abigail extended both arms as Deborah massaged the fragrant oil from her wrists to her elbows. She was correct. It completely transformed her usual perfume into something she'd never smelled before. "This is delightful. What is it?"

Pleased, she said, "It's a combination of spikenard and lavender, which complements the nardium you have on."

Abigail welcomed a new fragrance. She then fished the pouch from her pocket.

Weighing the coins in her hand, Deborah nodded. "I think this about does it."

It'd taken several years, a lot of men, many nameless, and most of her self-worth, but she filled the box.

Deborah opened the woven tapestry, inviting Abigail to join her in the other room.

This section of the shop was Abigail's favorite place to visit. She enjoyed seeing the blue, red, orange, and green colored oils in unique-shaped glass bottles that lined shelves from the ceiling to the floor. Some contained dried flowers, greenery, and precious stones in every shape and size.

"What're you going to do with the alabaster box?"

Without hesitation, Abigail responded proudly, "Purchase back my family's vineyard."

"That is wonderful." Deborah hugged her for the second time. Placing a hand under the younger woman's chin, she said, "Even with all that good news, you look as if you're carrying a substantial burden." Deborah patted the back of her hand. "Do you want to share what's heavy on your heart?"

Tears stung Abigail's eyes but never manifested enough to fall. Moist eyes were as close to crying as she'd ever gotten since saying goodbye to her grandfather.

"When my—" She paused to clear her throat. After exhaling several times, she continued. "Fourteen years ago today, my grandfather was out enjoying his leisurely walk in the vineyard when he suddenly stopped and gripped his chest. The workers later said his speech became garbled as he uttered, 'I can't feel my arm.' Then he died."

Deborah never moved her hand from Abigail's. The warmth of her touch was comforting. A breeze caused the fragrances to stir, but sadness dulled Abigail's senses.

"Afterwards, the Romans took everything away—they stole the only life I knew."

Chapter Four

Preparation

The house did as it was designed to do—stand out from its surroundings. Exotic flowers grew in the gardens ensuring endless bouquets for the dozens of ornate vases. Every pillow, window covering, and cushion were woven using the world's most exemplary tapestries. Its owner demanded excellence, and today, his expectations were nearly unobtainable. Servants almost tripped over each other as they frantically hurried from room to room.

"Everyone, stop what you are doing and come to the living area." Simon's voice boomed, causing feet to shuffle in his direction, followed by complete silence instantly.

Running his index finger over the table, the Pharisee yelled, "Look at this dust. The Teacher will be here tonight, and this isn't what I want greeting him." He raised both hands to his mouth and yelled. "Do you hear me?"

Heads bobbed their affirmation.

"Elizabeth, I want every fresh fruit, cheese, grain, and herb available."

Her brown eyes shifted to the crates of food at the entranceway. Simon knew how meticulous she was. She probably hadn't forgotten anything, but she'd check again to be sure.

"Is the calf roasting?" Simon asked the young man standing to his left.

"Two, sir, as well as pheasants and quail. We have dried fresh fish caught three days ago."

Simon slapped the cook's back in approval.

Squaring his shoulders, Simon strutted around the room. "This is the event of the decade. I want someone to guard the door and ensure only the most important guests are present. Let the commoners gather around the Teacher in the wilderness, not in my home."

He gave the house a final once-over. "The washbowls are to remain filled at all times," he ordered, looking down at the basins of water at the door's entrance. "Ensure that the water stays clean and fresh. Am I understood?"

A young lady with a slow right eye quickly ran over, carrying a pitcher of water. An older lady followed her with folded white linen towels and placed them on the small table near the door.

"Don't just stand there. Get busy," Simon barked. "The Teacher will be here in just a few hours. I want everything perfect." He clapped his hands, dismissing the staff.

Feet scampered, causing the room to sound like a stampede was taking place.

Chapter Five

Broken

"When my grandfather died, the Romans thought they were entitled to everything he owned—even me. As soon as the first soldier stormed into my room, I recognized the look. I'd seen it as a child after my parents died." Abigail couldn't believe she allowed the words to come from her mouth. She'd never spoken the account out loud. "After that day, he returned, again and again, bringing his friends."

Deborah stood to hug her younger friend.

Abigail touched her twitching eye with her right index finger. "By the sixth visit, I promised myself that I'd be in control of their comings and goings."

"I'm so sorry this happened to you. Adonai has a judgment place for those who abuse the orphan and widow. He will avenge the harm inflicted upon you."

Abigail shifted in her seat. "My grandfather used to recite the Torah to me each night. The sound of his voice gave me a sense of hope." She stiffened as she spoke. "Reality settled in, and I'm not so certain anymore that they contain life." She closed her eyes and massaged her throbbing temple. "At least not for me."

"There's *always* hope." She lowered her face to meet Abigail's gaze. "Moses said, 'I have waited for thy salvation, O Jehovah. As long as we have hope, we have life.'"

Abigail shook her head. She wished she still had faith, it would lead to hope, but hope unfulfilled resulted in a life of pain. Abigail vowed never to hurt again. She controlled her life even if it meant she suffered more.

"I'm told there is a Teacher..." Deborah allowed her words to trail off as if unsure whether Abigail would entertain the thought.

"I overheard the wife of Lucius's servant discussing it in the market." Her index finger rested between her nose and lip.

"Yes. My son was present. He followed behind as Yeshua—"

"Is that the Teacher's name?"

"According to Eli, it is. Some call him Jesus."

Abigail let the name slip through her lips several times. Each time she whispered Jesus, something tingled inside her heart. She stirred in a way that felt foreign to her.

"Friends of the captain came and said to Him, 'My master says you don't have to go to all this trouble. I'm not that important.'"

Abruptly dropping her hands to her side, Abigail stared at her feet. "If a centurion who builds synagogues is unworthy to stand before Him, He'd never be caught dead in the presence of someone as unclean..."

"As I was saying," Deborah continued. "He said, 'I'm too

embarrassed to have you in my home or for me to be in your presence. If you but say the word, Master, I know that my servant will be made whole.'"

"Are you saying as He spoke, He healed Abe?" Abigail recalled the story her cousin had once shared. "Yet another example of the water being stirred and someone was getting to it before I am able."

"What do you mean?"

"Nothing." Abigail collected the alabaster box. "Thank you for the tea and for keeping this safe for me. I must leave now."

Before Deborah could protest, Abigail walked out of the tent.

She kicked at a rock on the path. "Adonai blessed Sarai with Isaac, Job with health, and Solomon with wisdom." She looked at her hands. "And I have lain on my back for years to earn what? The ability to purchase what should already be mine."

"Micah," a man shouting across the path startled her, and she nearly dropped her treasure. "Are you on your way to Simon's? I heard the Teacher is there."

For the second time in mere moments, she nearly dropped her prized possession.

Turning to respond, "Simon the Pharisee? I didn't know, but of course I will be there. Shall we walk together?"

Abigail's feet had a mind of their own. She moved as if in a trance.

* * *

People were everywhere, making it difficult to see who was coming or going. Lowering her shawl to cover her face, Abigail entered and quickly washed her feet, then positioned herself near the far end of the table. Abigail was thankful for the new oils Deborah had allowed her to sample. It hid her typical fragrance enabling her to move about the room more freely though she deliberately avoided eye contact with anyone.

The crowd was too preoccupied with stories floating throughout the group to notice her.

A man who reminded Abigail of her grandfather whispered, "I heard He touched the coffin of a young man in Nain, and the boy came to life, got out the coffin, and hugged his mother."

"I heard he waved his hands over the water, and two brothers who were fishing caught so many fish, their boat almost sank," said a young man who looked to be in his late teenage years.

A burly man with a thick beard and a weather-worn face spoke up. "I was there." He reminded Abigail of her clients. "A nearby boat assisted with the catch, and it too almost sank."

With each testimony, her soul yearned to know more. She also felt a sense of sorrow at the thought Jesus would never pause to look at someone like her, let alone talk to her.

Then she shuddered as if doused in ice water. Tiny bumps covered Abigail's body. She rubbed both arms just as Jesus entered the room. Abigail recalled the words her grandfather said to her each night, "And he will be called Wonderful Counselor, Mighty God, Everlasting Father, Prince of Peace." Her chest heaved. She could hardly breathe.

Abigail, I heard people are healed at the pool of Bethesda.

She looked as Jesus reclined and recalled all the men who had come into her home. *I clean my clients' feet upon entering my home and they are sinners, yet—,* she thought to herself. Before she could comprehend what was taking place, her feet moved for the second time as if they had a mind all their own.

* * *

Of the greatness of his government and peace, there will be no end.

Abigail found herself reliving every hurt, pain, offense, abuse, and death that had ever afflicted her. The tears started in her soul and erupted into a waterfall.

* * *

The crowd audibly gasped as her tears soaked the Teacher's feet. They watched as she broke the box and poured it upon his feet. The fragrance filled the room.

Mortified, Simon glared in total disbelief. *Most surely, He isn't a prophet, or He'd know what manner of woman it is whose defiled hands are upon his body.*

She sobbed uncontrollably. As tears fell, they mingled with the oil. She kissed Jesus' feet then wiped them with her hair. She repeated this again and again, oblivious to the seemingly blatant disrespect. Completely fed up, he opened his mouth to speak.

"Simon." Jesus' tone caused him to swallow his harsh words. Everyone stopped gawking at the woman and focused their attention on him.

Abigail froze with fear. *How had she gotten on her knees? What was that fragrance? Did she break her box?*

Jesus placed a hand on her shoulders to prevent her from moving. "I want to share a story with you."

Oh, really? You have something to tell me? He jutted his chin out in defiance. Everyone had witnessed the harlot at the feet of Jesus.

Now Simon would go down in history as the man who exposed the greatest farce of all time. Crossing his arms across his chest, he said, "Speak, I'm listening."

"Two men were in debt to a banker. One owed five hundred silver pieces, the other fifty." Jesus paused, then continued. "Neither of them could pay up, and so the banker canceled both debts. Which of the two would be more grateful?"

All eyes looked Simon's way.

He shrugged at first. What did this have to do with the disgusting offense that had just played out? Then he cleared his throat and answered. "I suppose the one who was forgiven the most."

"That's right," said Jesus.

"But what does this have to do with me?" he snapped. "I am indebted to no one. I own everything I possess."

Turning his attention to the woman but still directing his words to Simon, Jesus asked, "Do you see this woman?"

Do I? I have been wondering if it is you who didn't see her. Simon nodded but said nothing.

"I came into your home, you provided no water, but she rained tears on my feet and dried them with her hair."

Simon shot his servants a stern glance, causing them to cringe.

Jesus continued, "You gave me no greeting, but from the time I arrived, she hasn't quit kissing my feet. You provided nothing for freshening up, but she has soothed my feet with perfume."

The Pharisee stumbled as it hit in his chest. He fell back on a chair and sulked as everyone stared at him. Simon had failed as the owner of the house. He had invited Jesus to come into his home. He was content to host the event but hadn't rendered the guest's an appropriate level of hospitality and care.

"Impressive, isn't it?" Jesus resumed speaking. "She was forgiven many, many sins, and so she is visibly grateful. If the forgiveness is minimal, the gratitude is minimal."

The noise in the crowd was deafening. Did Jesus say she has been forgiven? Who but Jehovah can forgive?

Abigail was utterly flabbergasted. When she lifted her gaze to meet His, He said, "I forgive your sins."

Someone dropped a wine decanter. The clay shattered as the plum-colored liquid flowed across the floor. "This is complete blasphemy."

Several guests stormed out of the home as they shouted, "Who does He think He is? God?"

Jesus spoke over the noise of the crowd. "Daughter, your faith has saved you. Go in peace."

The waters of Abigail's overflowed and spilled out in the form of tears. An angel hadn't touched her. Instead, the Son of God did.

1 Peter 5: 8 reads, "Be sober [well balanced and self-disciplined], be alert and cautious at all times. That enemy of yours, the devil, prowls around like a roaring lion [fiercely hungry], seeking someone to devour."

Chapter Six

Who Am I?

Like so many of you, I've walked through the brutal flames of adversity and snatched back my promises. At times, I lacked the necessary wisdom to possess them entirely, but I never stopped believing in the miraculous, even in my shortcomings. In the darkest of seasons, God's love, mercy, grace, and forgiveness protected me. The best way to share who I am is to tell you how I got my name.

All three of my grandmother's minor children became parents within a single nine-month period of time. Between December 1963 and June 1964, my cousins Jamese, Patrice, and I were born. Can you imagine being a single mother in a new state and each of your three underage children gave you a grandchild—within nine months? Talk about challenges. There would come a time when I asked my mother how I, the third granddaughter, was named after my grandmother.

"While I was pregnant with you, my mother still battled alcoholism. She'd tried unsuccessfully to get my brother James or sister Althea to name their daughters after her. They both vehemently refused. When you were born, she was determined to have a namesake. She screamed, cried, and made a scene until I conceded."

That visualization caused me to smile. BigMa was very animated. I could only imagine what her theatrics might look like while intoxicated.

Now, Florenza. She would pronounce our name as if each syllable was a word. *Sit up straight.* For emphasis, she placed an index finger squarely in my back, the other index finger against my forehead, and aggressively pressed, causing my entire body to perfectly align as if being touched by a chiropractor. My grandmother was a force with which to be reckoned. She was not always kind, nurturing, or caring. Often, she created storms that left scars on the people who loved her most. Those wounds would take years to heal—if ever. It took me several decades before I came to terms with the wreckage some of her choices left in her wake. Thankfully, I eventually did.

The scraping sound of the chair across a rickey floor brought my attention back to the conversation. "So, what I hear you saying is, I got my name because my grandmother was loud and tipsy?" Allowing the thought to settle, I asked, "What name had you selected for me?"

Smiling as if she'd waited my entire life for me to ask that question, she said, "I had the most beautiful name picked out for you." My mother placed a hand near her neck as if clutching a pearl necklace, then exhaled for emphasis. "You were going to be named Shanay Elise."

That took a few minutes to digest. "Shanay Elise instead of Florenza Denise?"

She was sensing my hesitation. "Years ago, no one had that name. *You* would have been the first. Doesn't it sound so exotic? Shanay Elise." Nostalgia set in, and my mother traveled down Memory Lane. I envisioned she had traveled back in time to the day I was born. The look in her eyes caused me to think she was mentally rocking me in her arms the day I was born. I stood and hugged her tightly.

"I think the name is lovely, just not a name I'd ever associate with myself."

The name didn't die. My aunt Althea gave an altered version of it to her second-born daughter.

Insight was a gift my grandmother inherited from her mother and her mother before her. As a powerful humanitarian, she used her voice to make changes in the prison system, foster care system, and courts. She paved the way for domestic violence victims to receive financial compensation to live independently. I came to a better understanding of who she was as a complete person.

My grandmother taught me to trust God and walk fully in my spiritual gifts. This confidence allows me to walk through doors others might view as closed; to see a rainstorm in a cloudless sky; to walk on water even though I don't know how to swim. My mother gave me life, but my grandmother gave me the power to dream. She recognized and developed in me gifts and talents that mandated I nurture them.

Something powerful occurs in a child's life when someone believes in them—they dare to believe in themselves.

"There's sometimes a tugging feeling you get to push further when you aren't being challenged enough or when things get too comfortable."

— Criss Jami, Killosophy

Chapter Seven

Drips of Water

John Adams High School was located on the east side of Cleveland, Ohio. The school served ninth through twelfth grades with an enrollment of ninety-eight percent minority races. Although the student-teacher ratio was about seventeen to one, only ten percent of the students were proficient in math and twelve percent in reading. John Adams would not be a place one might attend when interested in higher education; it was simply where the kids in our neighborhood went Monday through Friday. I, on the other hand, had my eyes on a higher target. Nothing less than a Master's degree would do. But first, I needed to survive high school.

The bell rang out a warning, causing feet to double-step. Being late to class was not an option. Not when the administration fully enforced corporal punishment. No one wanted to find themselves palms out, bracing against the hallway walls, butt tilted upward to receive swats from a two-inch board firmly gripped by an angry, underpaid, overworked educator.

"Who the hell does she think she is?" The words slipped past the black-lined lips of a high school tormentor as she rocked her weight back and forth on her dirty Sketcher sneakers. She thrust her hands into the pockets of a pink plastic see-through jacket. Her makeup made her look like she was auditioning to be Elvira: Mistress of the Dark, the horror-movie hostess known for super black eyeliner, lipstick, painted nails, and clothes. The only difference was, Elvia turned her freakish looks into a billion-dollar industry. This girl most likely didn't have two nickels to rub together to make a dime. Who was I kidding? Neither did I. Like I said, not exactly the best neighborhood.

Necks snapped in the direction of her stares and settled upon their target, little ole me. "Who wears suits and pumps to high school? She ain't no teacher."

Normally, I would've paused to respond, but not after the warning bell has already sounded. They weren't worth it, but that doesn't mean I didn't make a mental note of the encounter.

As I settled at the front of the class, I heard sighs of relief from those seated before the screech of the final bell. No one wanted to be in the halls after the last bell. No one.

"Ouch. Why are you hitting me so hard?" Screams echoed down the halls, testifying that someone hadn't made it to their desk in time. Teachers masterfully remained silent for a full three minutes following the bell as a form of mental torture.

That could be you.

Glancing around the overcrowded room, I saw emotionless faces that reminded me of late-night zombie television shows. The blank stares suggested many survived their form of abuse at home. Everyone goes through their hell. Some have a way of masking the scent of smoke better than most. None more than I.

After enduring an hour of boring diatribe from an educator who hated her occupation, the last bell of the day rang. I quickly made my way to the cafeteria; I was a member of the booster team. It wasn't as glamorous as being a cheerleader or on the step team, but it allowed me to remain at school later and attend sporting events; every minute at school was sixty seconds less of being at home. There are no free passes. Even brief episodes of independence came with a fee.

Those who fight to maintain authenticity pay the price. For me, it came in the form of endless bullying. I preferred to hang around guys—less drama, more chillin'. Since I wasn't interested in hooking up, guys enjoyed my company. They, too, liked being drama-free.

Rehearsals sounded more like lynch mobs. Cheers, that should have said, "KILL Kill the Eagles. Kill the Eagles," were instead, "KILL Kill Florenza. Kill Florenza." If girls understood how unattractive insecurities and jealousy were, they would curb it.

One particular time, their taunting wasn't only verbal assaults. That day, they would throw fists. Only then did I utilize all my inner hostility and pain and use it as a weapon.

"Hey, don't think you're going just to walk away from us." My challenger felt empowered since her posse was there, egging her on.

"Listen, I don't have beef with you. I'm not sure what your problem is, but I'm not it." I continued walking towards the door.

"You heard me talking to you." My foot stopped midair as I felt a firm grip on my left shoulder. "Yesterday, you said you wouldn't fight me because..." She snapped her fingers and turned to her crew before completing her sentence. "Because you were wearing a suit. That don't look like no suit to me."

If possible, my gaze would have burned holes into the hand that was violating my personal space. Instead, I lifted the unwelcome paw from my body and turned to walk out of the building. They followed. Seeing the crowd develop out on the sidewalk breathed new energy into their quest for a fight.

Realizing I had limited options, I thrust my shoulders back and tilted my chin upward. "What y'all ain't gonna do is jump me." I glared at each of them one by one. "So, you can line up..."

"Did she just say we could line up?"

This amazon had nothing to do with anything other than being an all-out bully. That was why I'd made up my mind she'd go last.

Not fazed one bit by the interruption, I continued as if she hadn't said a word. "I'll take you one at a time. When I get to you"—I threw my head back, staring up at the ringleader for emphasis, not the least bit intimidated by her size or height. "Then we'll keep going till one of us gets tired. And it won't be me."

I half-heard someone yelling. Then my vision narrowed so much. It nearly went black. I channeled every ounce of pain my one-hundred-and-twenty-pound body had stored up during my fifteen years on Earth.

Somewhere in the back of my mind, I envisioned the scene from *The Christmas Story* where Ralphie pummeled that bully. The only difference, I had no tears, and there was not one bully but an entire line of them. Come hell or high water. I was in for the win because—I can't swim.

While wailing on the first female, someone snatched me by my collar. Thinking it was the group trying to attack me all at once, I turned, ready to unleash my fury. It was a man I'd never seen before. My focus sharpened, and I realized several cars had stopped. The blonde hair, blue-eyed thirty-something-year-old had jumped out of his car to break up the catfight.

"Get your hands off of me. You don't know me." I felt spit forming in the corners of my mouth. I had always cringed when seeing that happen in others.

"What're you doing?" he shouted over my screams.

"They"—my arms flailed in a wide circle. "All jumped me." I poked my chest hard enough to break the skin. He stood there looking dumbfounded.

I lurched at my previous target, intent on finishing the Job. "I didn't start this fight. But I plan to end it."

One thing I knew for sure was you never just wound the target. You always go in for the kill. Wounded animals come back meaner. I didn't plan on having this encounter again.

He yanked back my collar for the second time. This time, the crowd dispersed, and I eventually made my way home. I'd have to deal with it another day.

* * *

Yeah, I thought as I recalled those haters' nasty comments while walking the few miles to my house. *My life should be yours. Then you'd see how much of a chameleon I am. All of you fools fell for the hype.*

The grass always appears to be greener across the street, and everyone wants to reside there. No one considers the cost of upkeep or that the lawn could be over a septic tank. Even worse, it could be AstroTurf—totally fake.

No matter how hard I tried, I still managed to have issues at school. Trouble has a way of finding some folk. If I stepped up to them or even tried to draw attention my way, I'd take full blame. But I didn't. The school wasn't an inconvenience to me like it was for others. It was my haven. Six hours a day, Monday through Friday, I could escape and be a kid. I could never understand how some squandered such a beautiful gift. Even teachers who hated their jobs appreciated a student who *wanted* to be in class and tried to put forth an effort. To me, that was a win-win. When I couldn't physically escape the challenges of home life, I became lost within the pages of a book.

Unfortunately, there would come a time when even the best of reading couldn't provide an escape and when school was no longer a sanctuary.

Chapter Nine

Pamphlets

The walk home was usually a pleasant stroll. I'd made friends with many of the families along the way. I'd wave to neighbors as I passed by; even petted the occasional dog that bolted to a fence. My favorite thing to do was to visit the corner store and buy candy. I always purchased enough for myself and my siblings. Sharing wasn't optional. But the previous fight had put me in a no-shopping mood. I wouldn't be going home with my usual bounty of a few packs of Now-n-Laters, Munch 'um chips, Sugar Mamas, a handful of Slo Poke Lollypops, and a few Astro Pops if they had them.

"Hey, girl, where are you going looking all fine?" The slick-talking boy trying to be a man looked at me like he was staring at a smothered pork chop on a plate. "Come over here, let me holla at you."

Holla at who? Boy, you're still living in your momma's basement. No life. No money. No future. Chile, please.

My energy only allowed the words to surface in my head; they ran out of gas before they could reach my lips. I sucked my teeth and kept on stepping.

Whoever coined the phrase cat-call for this inappropriate form of greeting is just as guilty. Women aren't cats, and we deserve to be treated with respect. But I knew why he, and others like him, were on the prowl. I was known as the *cute virgin*, and it garnered a lot of attention from the neighborhood hunters.

Where I lived wasn't a *bad* neighborhood, but it wasn't Bel Air either. My family had moved so many times by this point that I'd lost count. My mother was a hard worker. Unfortunately, my father had a gambling addiction which interfered with her ability to pay bills. Rare were the Fridays he didn't visit her place of employment demanding her to cash her check and give him the money. When the rent wasn't paid, the U-Haul followed. Every year, it seemed like I was attending another school. I actually attended two high schools, though this was by choice. Attending Jane Addams Vocational High School was equivalent to winning the lottery. Different schools meant being the new kid all over again and re-igniting the never-ending fight to fit in. Mine was the battle to remain authentic and not conform.

Most years, I was victorious, though there were a few moments of defeat. Home, however, was where the lines blurred, the colors soon blending into a shade similar to dirty paint water that became the palate from which I colored life.

"You hear me talking to you. For the record, you ain't that fine."

Can you believe that fool was still standing at the chain link fence hollering down the block?

Fighting at school, surviving the streets. What was next?

* * *

"Necie."

My mother called my name as soon as I walked into the house. There was an edge to her voice. *How had she heard about the fight already? The streets do talk.*

My mind raced to connect the dots. The ability to perceive what was coming my way and prepare my response was my superpower. Lately, I was behaving as though affected by mental Kryptonite. I desperately searched to find the location of that glowing green stone. I paused and breathed in three deep breaths, something my grandmother had taught me—one for the Father, one for the Son, and the third for the Holy Ghost.

During my final exhale, the answer came to me. I recalled the account of my mom getting into a worse fight. Only, she had her brother make her brass knuckles with exposed nails. I gagged as I heard how she shredded the girl's face and nearly took her sight away.

"Scared people do strange things," she'd told me. "I was always bullied. I finally got tired of it and had to defend myself." My mother paused and blinked back tears. "I wish that I hadn't gone for her face."

With a faraway look, she added, "I never had to worry about anyone else messing with me after that, though."

The ends justified the means.

That's it. I would just quote my mom and say, *I didn't start the fight, but I did end it.*

As I turned the corner, I saw her sitting at the kitchen table. The room was small but tidy. The golden stove and the matching refrigerator were on the right-hand wall; against the other wall was the empty sink. The table was situated in the center of the room, flanked by four yellow floral vinyl chairs. A bottle of Alaga syrup and homemade hot sauce were on the table, signifying dinner would be fried chicken and homemade biscuits. Thinking of the spices in that hot concoction—a recipe handed down from the Geechee side of the family—opened my sinuses up and made my nose run.

My mother's once youthful face now showed signs of wear and tear. Hair that was always meticulously styled was now slightly messy. Her eyes were red and puffy. She repeatedly swiped her right hand across her tiny button nose as she sniffed.

Rushing to her side. "Mommy, it's okay." Wiping tears from her eyes, I fought back the need to purge my soul with a good cry. The reversal of roles was no longer a strange experience. From the moment I entered this world, I was the confidant, supporter, friend, a lifeline to my fifteen-year-old mom. What else would I be? Her hurt originated from such a deep dark place; it took my birth to bring in light. There was a fee to being depended upon so heavily. Soon, I'd have to pay that price.

* * *

If I had to define my life, one word would've come to mind—crypt. Beautiful and pristine on the outside, decrepit and rotting within. "What happens in this house ..." If you can finish the sentence, I see you too know the rules of engagement. Why is it that we're more comfortable pretending to be happy around people who could care less while living in misery with those who claim to love us? All smiles on the outside while suffocating within. I'd mastered the art of pretense.

Life was measuring, mixing, stirring, and prepping me for something that felt a bit off-kilter. I couldn't quite understand it but sensed a storm was brewing.

* * *

Dangling from her taupe painted nails were random pamphlets—all of which I'd seen before. "I found these under my pillow this morning."

My shoulders slumped as my gaze turned downwards. I was not embarrassed but rather because I felt the need to bring home anti-drug flyers with information on treatment facilities specializing in addiction. I had made my way to the nurse's office at school after discovering paraphernalia around the house, those tell-tell signs something wasn't right: tiny tin foil packages, white residue magically appearing on tables and mirrors, rolled-up dollar bills, and locked doors.

Hot tears stung my eyes, yet I dared one to fall. This ordeal was not my fault.

"Why do I keep finding these everywhere?" Her question drew me back to the conversation. "Under my pillow, in my drawers, in the kitchen cabinets." She dropped them on the table and waited for my eyes to meet hers. Minutes felt like hours.

Growing tired of staring at the nicked linoleum floors, I raised my chin and met the glare of a stranger. Strongholds now controlled the earthly home that housed my best friend, my confidant, my mother. Although naturally petite, drugs stole what little weight she once possessed. Her favorite dress hung on her body like a wire garment on a hanger, and dilated pupils stared from hollow holes. Addiction provided a false sense of being invincible. It also blinded individuals to the need for salvation.

My mother's life hadn't always been easy. The truth be told, it was downright disrespectful. A lifetime of abuse had taken its toll. Yet, with all that life threw at her, she never lost her smile—until now. Not wanting my words to add weight to her already heavy burden, my response was simple, "I just want you to be well."

The sadness in her expression was a representation of the choices that brought us to this place. As her firstborn, I witnessed each struggle, pain, onslaught, and conflict. I was also present for the episodes of joy, happiness, and laughter that occurred during the countless mother-children game nights. Her current war made it virtually impossible for her to separate fiction from reality. As the lines blurred, it ushered in confusion that threatened to end both our lives. She was drowning, and I couldn't swim, and we were both in the center of the ocean.

Her silence was my invitation to leave.

Over time, even tiny drops of water will eventually fill up a bucket and force it to overflow.

Chapter Ten

Tipping Point

Reaching for the cordless house phone on the kitchen wall, I headed upstairs. I needed to talk; I was uncertain as to whom. I thought to call my aunt, then changed my mind.

My aunt would know what to do. She was a year or so younger than my mom and equally as beautiful. Her peach skin, doe-like eyes, and huge smile were electrifying. Her laugh silenced the room, inviting everyone to enter her joy. She, too, battled addiction, but it never seemed to threaten her life. At least that's what she'd have us all to believe.

She'd once applied to Julliard and was accepted. She would make paper dolls and design their clothes as if they were miniature models. Her makeup skills matched any professional makeup artist in New York City. She also had a way of listening that allowed the speaker to find a path to discovering an answer independently.

The wall leading up the stairwell contained portraits of smiling faces that mocked me as I ascended. My home started feeling like a prison. My body felt heavier with each step. Despair replaced determination; security became profound sadness, and it gripped my soul. The pain had nothing to do with the earlier fight; this was spiritual.

Dropping the bookbag on the floor near my bed, I went to the bathroom to wash my hands. Only then did I see my face and remembered the scuffle. *Who was that guy that snatched me by my collar?* There I was, protecting myself, and I still got accosted. I laughed, thinking I had to be wailing on the girl for him to snatch me and not her. Maybe I packed a more powerful punch than I thought. Who knew? Up until that moment, my words had kept me out of trouble, sort of.

"Your mouth is going to write a check that your butt can't cash," my aunt had once told me. She was one of my favorite people in the world.

Opening the door to the medicine cabinet, I pushed past rows of narcotics, searching for a Band-aid for my arm. Call it a cosmic shift, a temporary possession, or mental break, but something maligned. When closing the cabinet, the reflection staring back at me was not my own. Fear gripped my heart.

In disbelief, my shaking fingers touched the glass, hoping that whatever was occurring would right itself, but it didn't. Staring back at me was my mother's reflection. Tiredness replaced my youthful hue. The weight of my day came crashing in like a tidal wave. How many times had I cried? The answer was fewer times than I have fingers, yet now the tears wouldn't stop flowing.

Darkness reached out its hideous tentacles and gripped me, making it difficult to maintain my balance. I felt temporarily possessed and incapable of controlling my actions. An emotional avalanche came cascading upon my soul.

Turning the tops of each bottle, I emptied then lined all the pills along the edge of the sink. For a split second, I considered flushing them or allowing them to fall down the drain. Upon regaining my composure, I collapsed on the top step and noticed the phone in my hand.

Shaky fingers punched in a number I'd called many times before. Only this time, it was for me and not my mother.

"Suicide hotline, please hold."

Where might someone turn for assistance when the people designated to help put you on hold? At that time, I was clueless, vulnerable, and in imminent danger.

Returning to the bathroom, I turned the silver knob on the faucet until water flowed. *Please hold.* Cupping one hand to collect water, I alternated gulping water and swallowing pills until they were all gone. Then I went to lie down.

A floating sensation took over my body as all sounds faded. The weight of my lids caused my eyes to close—the end.

Not exactly, although I have no way of confirming what happened next beyond a gut instinct. Angels appeared and lifted my body off the bed, moving each foot until I stood in the kitchen again. Based on the aromas coming from the stove, approximately two or three hours must have passed. *Wasn't it darker outside than when I last looked?*

My mother stared at me as if she could read my mind. She opened her mouth, but no sounds came out. I then heard myself say, "Guess what I did?" I opened my hands to reveal the bottles.

Then everything went black.

* * *

Ear-piercing bleeps caused me to open my lids only to experiences immense pain from the blinding light. I closed them as quickly as I had opened them. A sense of discomfort caused me to reach up and grasp my right arm. I followed the tube a few inches as it trailed down my right side and through cold metal rails.

"She's awake," a familiar voice shouted from my right-hand side. Slowly I eased open my eyes to allow my pupils to adjust. Faint scents of antiseptic and food wafted through the air. I became nauseated and barely turned my head towards the floor before vomit erupted like a volcano.

Without certainty, I'm unsure what else took place after opening my eyes. Everyone around me was joyful and praising God for what the doctors labeled a miracle. If it was *miraculous*, why did I feel like a failure?

* * *

A few weeks later, my mother stood at my bedroom door. "Necie, you should go outside and get some fresh air. You've been in the house for days."

Fresh air was the least of my desires, but I obliged. I found myself at the corner store.

"Where you been hiding out?" How is it that the same dude who was in his mother's front yard on the day of the fight would still be standing there? Perhaps, like a chained puppy, he was limited in where he could roam.

My grandmother always said common sense isn't so common. Somewhere, I felt her eyes rolling at the following idiotic decision I'd make. Rather than scoffing at the lewd remarks, I walked towards the source. It would prove to be a horrible decision. I seemed to be racking those up like wild cards in a game of Spades.

How often can time stand still for one person? More importantly, how many poor decisions could one person make before they learned the lesson? I hadn't even begun kindergarten in the school of life.

Far more than my virginity was taken that day. What little self-worth I had remaining also vanished. Before I could leave through the front door, his brother sprang from the sofa, grabbed me, pinned me down, and raped me. Initially, I thought the event had been a nightmare until several months later. I nearly died for the second time from an ectopic pregnancy.

While working as a Candy Striper at the local VA Hospital, I felt severe abdominal pains that caused me to double over in agony. I vaguely remember stumbling over to press the call button, alerting the head registered nurse to come quickly. By the time she arrived, I had passed out.

I awakened to a very handsome Caucasian doctor standing over me. In my stupor, I asked, "Am I in Heaven? Are you an angel?" He simply smiled and told me no. The doctor asked a few questions I must have answered because they sent me immediately to another non-military facility from there. The next doctor to enter the room was not as welcoming or friendly. She was an African American mid-thirties provider who simply announced, "You are pregnant, and the fetus is in your tubes. I will be performing emergency surgery to remove *it* and the fallopian tube. Do you have someone you'd like us to contact?"

Just like that, no comfort, no support, no compassion, just judgment, and condemnation.

My parents arrived, and with them came a slew of questions. "Whose is it?" "When did this happen?" "What were you thinking?" just to list a few of them.

At that time, I was too embarrassed to tell my parents about the assault, so I simply lied and said, "I don't know."

Although disappointed, they never asked anything further.

I went from being wounded to broken, which caused me to spiral downhill until I was utterly shattered. And that brutal rape would remain a secret that mercilessly gnawed at my soul until I penned this book. It became a form of emotional cancer that failed to heal. That summer, I became reckless.

Trees are easy to bend when they are young and frail. Unless repositioned early, they grow misaligned. Our hearts are the same. Hidden hurts can never heal.

Chapter Eleven

The Bus Stop

Romance is not my flavor. I never developed that trait. However, I love hearing couples share how they first met. Their story usually begins with, "Our eyes connected across the smoke-filled room, and it was love at first sight."

My courtship was no cookie-cutter, tissue-moment fairytale. My heart was still broken from the previous summer, and demons still lay beneath hidden pains and secrets masked by pretending smiles.

That all changed one frigidly cold day. At the bus stop, I stood shuddering with my friend Eva. For those who've ever experienced winters in Ohio, your bones are already trembling at the mere thought.

The bus was late, it was frigid cold, and I had to deal with *slugs* driving by, hollering out the passenger side windows. The colder it got, the more frustrated I became. Then, a fair-skinned, toothy-grinned guy with thick black hair and a beard slowly drove by. He turned around. Yelling out his passenger window, "Where're you going?"

Looking up the road, I didn't see a hint of a bus. "School."

He looked at me as if I'd hit him.

Flippantly, I responded, "You got a problem with that? Where are you going?"

"What school do you go to?" He looked like he had won the *Golden Ticket*. "I'll take you."

Looking to my friend, Eva, who could've taken down a Cleveland Brown fullback if he got out of line, and she nodded that it was okay to tell him.

"We go to Jane Addams High School."

He reached across the seat and opened the passenger door. "Hop in, then. It's on my way."

Jumping into the backseat, I left the front free and clear for Eva.

The white Monte Carlo was well-kept, and that was a refreshing trait. Glancing up, I saw him staring at me from the rearview mirror.

"Keep your eyes on the road. We're riding on ice, dummy." I nearly screamed.

En route, I learned his name was Trefus, but he preferred to be called Lee, and like me, he was seventeen years old. I also discovered that his cousin, Tammy, and I attended the same school.

We arrived early, and as I was saying thank you and getting out of the car, he asked for my phone number.

"Eva, he wants your phone number," I called over my shoulder.

She wasn't playing around. She'd already made her way into the building; it was chilly. I didn't blame her.

Thinking for a few moments, I brushed off the snowflakes that quickly accumulated on my notebook before snatching out a piece of paper. "Why not? Here you go." Fishing a pen out of my purse, I scribbled my digits down and passed them to him.

He grinned like he'd won the lottery. I did too. Car rides were a lot better than packed smelly buses, and as long as I had Eva, I was safe.

As soon as I walked inside the building, I found Tammy and asked a million questions. Something about him captured my attention. Not quite hooked, but I was intrigued. As soon as I mentioned his name, she said, "Girl, he's one of the good ones." Curiosity turned into interest, and this set into motion the beginning of our courtship. Soon I learned that although it was the first day I'd seen him, it wasn't the first time he'd seen me.

That summer, Trefus watched from his bedroom window as I walked by his house on my way to work. I was a nurse's aide at the local Veteran Affairs Hospital. He'd later confess that he told himself, *I'm going to marry that woman.* When he saw me standing at the bus stop, he thought it was an answer to prayer.

Marriage wasn't a part of my vocabulary. I had plans: college, law school, then a seat on the Supreme Court. None of that required marriage. It did, however, necessitate hard work, dedication, and a purpose-driven focus. My amazingly gorgeous looks smote Trefus. Who could blame him? But he had a life planned out as well, and initially, it didn't include me.

He'd tried to escape by moving to California to live with his older brother. The fast-pasted lifestyle proved to be too much, and he found himself back home joining the Navy under their delayed-entry program. Previous stupid choices caused that ship to sail. Seeing his struggle, I called an Army recruiter friend and told him I had someone who needed to join. That's the story of how Trefus Lee became Private Lee. He followed his dreams and left Ohio. I set out for Michigan State in pursuit of becoming a judge, and that was that.

You already know this isn't how that story ended.

Chapter Twelve

Engagement

I thank my God every time I think of you. Philippians 1:3

Jewelry stores make a lot of money from commercials depicting partners getting down on one knee, emotionally choked up, brandishing a ring while asking those four words: "Will you marry me?"

Not me. I got a phone call that went like this.

"Hey, Necie. Guess what I just heard?"

"What?"

"The Army will give me more money if I'm married."

"What's that got to do with me?"

By age eighteen, I'd been earning an income for as long as I could remember. Babysitting jobs, summer work programs, working at the neighborhood store in exchange for food items, sewing, doing hair. Now the time had come for me to branch out. However, my college dreams bottomed out when my student loan packet didn't cover summer attendance, and I found myself in debt. I planned to return home and do what I did the best, work my behind off.

But maybe this was my Plan B. I reconsidered my previous response. "Could we live in Germany?" I asked.

"Yes."

"Deal," I answered before my mind could pose more questions. I needed to distance myself from those painful memories that were slowly surfacing, threatening to choke out any semblance of an ever life.

"My brother is on his way to take you downtown to get the license. I'll be home this weekend."

You read that correctly. My brother-in-law drove me to get a marriage license, and four days later, we were standing in Lee's mother's living room surrounded by the few family members I told. Standing before his pastor, we said, "I do."

Those who've seen the sparse photos always comment on my facial expression.

Many have asked, "What was going through your mind?" Stating that I looked as serious as a heart attack.

"During the vows, I was daring Pastor Winston to say the word *obey*."

"Did he?" is always the question. The answer is he dared not.

The first few years of our marriage, we were like two kids playing a game to which we hadn't yet learned the rules and regulations.

The desire to maintain what I thought was the perfect Christian image caused me to struggle. All the while, at the same time, I worked desperately to keep my secrets hidden. I felt that God had heard me when I asked for forgiveness in the depth of my heart, but I had a hard time loving myself. Is it possible to love others as you should when you don't love yourself first?

Eventually, I would learn the answer to this question.

"Nothing is more creative... nor destructive... than a brilliant mind with a purpose."

— Dan Brown, Inferno

Chapter Thirteen

The Move

True to my husband's promise, we packed our bags and moved to Germany. I'd read Abraham and Sarah's journey numerous times in the Bible of how they trusted God and followed as He directed. Somewhere in my soul, I felt that we were embarking on our faith walk. We joked that we were missionaries at the government's expense. There was a vast world outside of Ohio, and I planned to see as much of it as I could.

As the plane landed, something nearly unfathomable happened. I can only describe it by saying, "My soul felt like it had returned home." I know. Germany isn't what you expected to read. One would think stepping foot on African soil would garner such a response, not Germany. But that's what occurred.

The military life proved to be a perfect fit for me. I never got bored with the constant moving, whether we were someplace exotic or in a mundane location. The challenges were as diverse as our addresses. Along with them came the sense of never being settled. I learned that I would not have a career and was alright with it. I vowed to make every Job an adventure.

* * *

"Florenza Lee."

Standing, I smoothed my pink linen skirt and gently tugged the edges of the matching jacket. My stride was confident and sure. I had toiled for hours over my resume, and it was perfect. Being more than qualified for the entry-level position at the Base Exchange gave me inner confidence.

"Yes, ma'am."

Her piercing blue eyes glared up and down my petite frame. I checked to ensure each button on my jacket was securely closed before extending my arm. "It is a pleasure to meet you."

Her limp right hand was my first indication this interview wasn't going to proceed as expected. She turned on her sensible rubber-soled shoes and, with long strides, walked towards an open door. Matching her pace, my heels clicking on the tile floors. We reached the door a nanosecond apart. Her expression revealed she thought she'd lost me. My smile matched her shock.

"Frau Lee is here to see you." I heard a *humph* as she turned to walk away.

In her grey tweed jacket and wool skirt, Frau Maclemar looked like a cold winter day. I second-guessed my decision to wear pastels instead of a more business-appropriate shade of dull. She nodded in approval. "It's a pleasure to meet you, Frau Lee. Please have a seat." Her accent was thick, and her shake firm. Her presence showed a lot more promise,

Her office lacked all personal touches, but it was tidy—every item in its place. The images on the walls were of water and mountain scenes. It could stand to have fresh-cut flowers, or a pillow tossed here or there, something to liven it up. Then again, they weren't paying me to come in as the interior designer. It would behoove me to stay in my lane.

The interview went well, and within an hour, they offered me the position. A few weeks later, I learned they had already pre-selected me; the interview was a mere formality. The name Florenza Lee had confused everyone, especially the female who had selected me. They expected someone Asian or white—not black.

The distance between work and home required I take two buses, a train, and a taxi. During that time, I read the Word of God. It felt like I was reuniting with a long-lost friend. With each book read, I felt my faith grow and strengthen. When I read Luke 7:36-50, I felt overwhelmed with joy.

One of the Pharisees asked Jesus to eat with him, and He went into the Pharisee's house [in the region of Galilee] and reclined at the table.

Now there was a woman in the city who was [known as] a [a] sinner; and [b]when she found out that He was reclining at the table in the Pharisee's house, she brought an alabaster vial of perfume, and standing behind Him at His feet, weeping, she began wetting His feet with her tears and wiped them with the hair of her head, and [respectfully] kissed His feet [as an act signifying both affection and submission] and [c]anointed them with the perfume.

Now when [Simon] the Pharisee who had invited Him saw this, he said to himself, "If this Man were a prophet, He would know who and what sort of woman this is who is touching Him, that she is a [notorious] sinner [an outcast, devoted to sin]."

Jesus, answering, said to the Pharisee, "Simon, I have something to say to you."

And he replied, "Teacher, say it."

"A certain moneylender had two debtors: the one owed him five hundred [d]denarii, and the other fifty. When they had no means of repaying [the debts], he freely forgave them both.

So which of them will love him more?"

Simon answered, "The one, I take it, for whom he forgave more." Jesus said to him, "You have decided correctly." Then turning toward the woman, He said to Simon, "Do you see this woman? I came into your house [but you failed to extend to Me the usual courtesies shown to a guest]; you gave Me no water for My feet, but she has wet My feet with her tears and wiped them with her hair [demonstrating her love]. You gave Me no [welcoming] kiss, but from the moment I came in, she has not ceased to kiss My feet. You did not [even] anoint My head with [ordinary] oil, but she has anointed My feet with [costly and rare] perfume.

Therefore I say to you, her sins, which are many, are forgiven, for she loved much; but he who is forgiven little, loves little." Then He said to her, "Your sins are forgiven."

Those who were reclining at the table with Him began saying,

"Who is this who even forgives sins?"

Jesus said to the woman, "Your faith [in Me] has saved you; go in peace
[free from the distress experienced because of sin]."

There on the bus ride, I heard the voice of a loving Savior beckoning my soul to surrender to Him. Rather than respond, *please, hold.* I answered yes and completely surrendered all of my hurt and pain to Christ.

Tears broke the grip of all of the weights and the sins that stood between He and me. The multiple suicide attempts, loss of my virginity, rapes, arms void of the children not born all came rushing back. Every futile effort to cover up the pain and the severe consequences flashed before me. While riding on that bus, I saw each of my failures not as something that separated me from Him but instead revealed my need for the One who loved me most.

To every thing there is a season, and a time to every purpose under the heaven:
Ecclesiastes 3:1 (KJV)

Chapter Fourteen

The Church

My husband and I have a knack for transforming mundane things into works of extravagance. Germany is a thrifter's dream. It isn't uncommon to see an entire house full of furniture ideally situated on the curb. The Europeans call this junking. Families who upgraded their homes would set their old furniture outside. I'm not talking about broken, unusable items. I mean showroom-worthy articles, including rugs, lamps, dishes, pots and pans, and more. Our first home mirrored images I'd only seen in magazines—all for free.

My husband excelled at work, and we embraced the European lifestyle. Each weekend, we'd ride our bicycles for miles, enjoying the countryside, eating at local cafes, and living every moment like tourists. We visited castles, and ancient vineyards, attended festivals and more.

One day while waiting for the second bus on my way to work, I looked up and saw a tall, smiling, caramel-complexion guy with a military-style haircut and a Bible in his hand...

"What verse are you reading?" I asked.

He glanced down then closed the book. "I was reading Psalms. Are you familiar with my Father's words?"

Am I?

As we awaited the bus, I learned that his name was Norman, and he attended a small church on the economy—meaning out in the German community and not on base. He invited me to attend and gave me his phone number. I felt that this was not a chance encounter, but God orchestrated. Later that night, I shared the information with my husband. We attended the following Sunday. The congregation was small but caring, and it felt right. We quickly found our place, and the Church House of Deliverance (CHOD) became our church home. God was the missing piece.

Continuing to pour over the Word of God so diligently caused my husband to think I was *losing it*. He later told me that I'd be sitting on the floor studying with various Bibles when he'd come home. Looking up, I saw him glancing back at me wide-eyed. Google didn't exist back then. Information had to be researched the old-fashioned way—by reading.

Authors such as Smith Wigglesworth, Watchman Nee, Oswald Chambers, and John Wycliffe captured my attention. I learned to navigate Dake's Annotated Bible, which should come with a disclaimer: *Warning. You can get lost for hours on end within these pages.*

I hadn't learned that there was a downside to knowledge; she seeks a place to plant seeds. I spoke of God's goodness to anyone and everyone. The more I shared, the more fruit I enjoyed. It wouldn't be long before my growth would upset the apple cart called the church. Only then did I discover my true strength.

*I know that thou canst do every thing, and that no
thought can be withholden from thee.*
                                        Job 42:2 (KJV)

Chapter Fifteen

Visions

Although I'd wrestle with my past at times, I did find peace in the presence of God's word. As a little girl, I had witnessed the power of God to perform miracles. That summer, when my life turned upside down, I lost the ability to see spiritually.

* * *

Laying in our master bedroom, I listened to my husband as he snored. Nothing, in particular, occurred that would cause me to be awake. But there I was, eyes wide open. Saying a prayer for my family, his, and our church, I closed my eyes. Then something shifted.

Although it had been a while, the familiarity was unmistakable—the presence of God. I waited for a word, revelation, truth. What I sensed was the need to open my eyes.

We had a traditional German-style bed—two full-size mattresses overlaying a king-size box spring. My husband slept with the white goose-down duvet tucked neatly under his chin. Feeling the space between the two mattresses under my right hip, I inched closer to my husband. This caused him to stir a bit. As he turned over on his left side, he rested his chin on my right shoulder. His breath was warm against my skin. He was next to me, and I felt safe.

Slowly opening my eyes, I saw something that sent shivers throughout my body. Goosebumps covered every surface of my skin.

Hideous creatures stood shoulder to shoulder. Not even in my nightmares could I have conjured them. I immediately closed my eyes and positioned my husband's right arm across my belly; I wrapped my left hand around his for support. As I squeezed my eyes shut, I heard in my heart, "Daughter, open your eyes."

Open my eyes? Did you just see what I saw? I will not open my eyes.

"Do you trust me?" God asked.

Hearing the question caused me to think of Adam in the Garden. A question that didn't require a response because God already knew the answer.

Of course. I trust you with my eternal life.

"Then, please. Open your eyes."

When I found the courage to be obedient, the same terrifying creatures as before were still there. Only this time, angelic beings were present. These were not the fat cherubs painted above fireplace mantels during Christmastime but mighty warriors. I couldn't see their faces because a pair of wings covered them, as well as another pair of wings outstretched beyond the room, and the third covered their feet.

Their hands held swords that glowed like liquid gold held at a forty-five-degree angle across their chests. They aligned themselves wingtip to wingtip, protecting me from the reach of the demons.

As I stared, these are the words I heard in my heart… "Demons will always be present. They walk back and forth, looking for individuals to consume and destroy. They temporarily rule the air. There will come a time when they will be cast into the Lake of Fire. Until then, between them and you are my angels. The blood of Jesus covers you. My Holy Spirit surrounds you and orders your steps. Nothing can come near you that hasn't first passed through my hands. Perfect love casts out all fear. Always walk in, my love."

A sense of boldness stirred in my heart, and I knew that it would be the beginning of me learning to trust God completely.

"Man is here for the sake of other men - above all for those upon whose smiles and well-being our own happiness depends."

— Albert Einstein

Chapter Sixteen

Training Weekend

With light brown eyes pleading for reconsideration, he said, "I want a baby."

"What?" I wasn't sure I'd heard my husband correctly.

"The other families at church all have kids. We should too," he said. "I want a baby."

That wasn't the first time we'd had the conversation. It'd been going on for a few years.

Despite my objections, I had to admit, seeing all the babies running around that storefront building did spark a maternal flame in my heart, which surprised me. I would have bet the farm that there wasn't even a pilot light in that space.

For a brief moment, I envisioned how a child conceived by the two of us might look. Of all that we were fortunate to possess, good genes were top of the list. No mistake, we would create intelligent, kind, and beautiful babies.

"When is the next time you go away for training?" I asked.

This got his attention. Since it was a completely different response than my usual, "Have you fallen and hit your head?"

Grinning from ear to ear, he practically did a happy dance. "I have a month-long training coming up soon."

"Pump your breaks. I didn't say we're going to make one right now." We both enjoyed a good laugh.

Trefus started pacing almost as if he was already in the delivery room. He indeed was ready to be a dad.

"Tell you what."

He looked my way, anticipation all in his expression.

I was scratching my chin with my index finger. "I'll stop taking my pills when you leave, and when you come home, you got one weekend to make it happen. Deal?"

My husband shook my hand as if he'd just received the keys to a mansion.

True to my word, I discontinued my birth control, and his first weekend home, we made a baby.

Chapter Seventeen

Lost

Seven months later, our church was in revival. My husband wanted to arrive early, so I chose to take the bus. Around two o'clock, I left the house, made my way to the bus stop, and waited. Then waited and waited some more.

Scanning the area, I didn't see a single bus. That was highly unusual. You could set your watch on the punctuality of German public transportation.

Thinking I could use the time to my advantage, I started walking to the next bus stop. I was seven months pregnant and could always use the extra exercise. When I arrived, I again waited, then repeated my earlier actions by walking to the next stop. After doing this a few times, it dawned on me—it was a German holiday, and the buses were running on the Sunday schedule. Somewhere in my mind, I thought it was a good idea just to keep walking.

The sidewalk eventually led to a wooded area that went under the highway. I don't wear watches, and cell phones weren't yet a thing, so I had no way of knowing how long I had been walking. The sun was starting to descend. I hadn't eaten or drank water, and the baby was pressing down on my bladder. I convinced myself it wasn't that much further. But I knew differently.

As I walked through the woods, I listened for the sound of anyone enjoying an evening stroll. Europeans love walking in the evening, and I was sure I'd see someone soon. My German wasn't as good as my husband's, but I could at least ask for directions. My belly looked like I was smuggling a toddler. I was sure to gain the pity of anyone passing by. But for several hours, I saw no one.

I'd be lying if I said I wasn't scared. The darker it became, the more terrified I became. And the sky darkened more.

The baby was doing summersaults on my bladder. I found a tree where I could at least shield my squat and relieve myself. Fear set in, and the back end released as well. I stood there, crying half from embarrassment and the other from worry. I was alone, lost, and worse. No one knew where even to begin to look had they realized I'd gone missing.

My entire body quaked with anxiety as I called out to God in anger. "I don't care about me, but please don't let my baby die." As soon as the words left my lips, something caught my attention. It moved quickly along the edge of the trees. My first thought was that it was a snake. I stood from my squatting position in preparation to flee. Then I saw it—a rabbit.

Something about the way it stared at me seemed otherworldly. Could the rabbit have heard my prayer? Could this be God's way of answering me, or did I imagine the entire thing? I was *not* hallucinating. The rabbit and I were in a staring contest.

"If you can understand me and you are staring as though you can, please show me how to get out of here." The sound of my voice was strange in my ears. I could only imagine what it might have sounded like had someone been in the woods with me.

"Gretchen, die Dame redet mit einem Hasen."

"Did you say she is talking to a rabbit?"

"Ja."

If talking to a bunny would save my baby's life, call me the rabbit whisperer.

"The greatest thing in this world is not so much where we stand as in what direction we are moving."
— Johann Wolfgang von Goethe

Chapter Eighteen

Back Door

As insane as it sounds, I followed that rabbit through the bushes and alongside a rocky path. Cradling my stomach tightly, we weaved between many trees and tall thorny bushes.

My ankles took a beating, but I kept moving for what seemed like an hour. It felt like we were going in circles, and just as I was about to sit down and give up, I heard music. Not just singing, I heard someone praising God in English. Rubbing the inside of my ears with my pointer fingers, I attempt to clear them out.

First, I'm being led around by a rabbit. Then I hear things. This can't be happening.

The bunny glanced back at me as if questioning why I'd stopped moving. It quickly jerked its head forward and then went underneath a tall bush. The thickness of it required that I press in backward. I didn't know what was lurking on the inside or other side, and I didn't want my stomach to be the first thing to find out. As I felt the branches clear, I turned and nearly fainted from disbelief. I was standing at the parking lot of the church. My church!

When I opened the back door, the bright light of the small room was a beautiful sight. I immediately walked over to the stainless-steel sink, retrieved a glass from the cabinet, and drank what felt like a gallon of water. Based on the digital clock on the wall, it had been nearly seven hours since I'd first stepped out of my house. Both baby and I were parched.

As I stood gulping water, one of the ladies glanced down at my scraped ankles and bleeding legs. Concern filled her eyes, and her lips parted to inquire about it. I waved off any questions and hugged her as I made my way to the small sanctuary. My husband was standing by the front door chatting with someone. His gaze followed me as I made my way to the podium. Praise erupted from my soul like lava from Mount St. Helen. I may have missed the service, but I didn't miss the revival.

After what seemed like an eternity, my husband made his way to the front, gently lifted me from the carpet, and escorted me to the small bathroom. Bracing my back against the wall, he removed several brown paper towels from the dispenser, wet them with warm water, and added soap. In silence, he lovingly washed away everything that had soiled my body, just as God had cleansed the stains from my soul.

While I was pouring out my praise to God, He reminded me of the vision of the angelic and demonic beings and reiterated He is always present to protect me. That night, he had used a rabbit to guide me through the woods and led me to my destination. I learned that God is my source, but He uses resources to bring His blessings to fruition. As long as we don't limit how God may move in our lives, He will continue to bless us.

While riding home, I saw just how far I had walked. I told Trefus about my journey and about the answer to the prayer that God sent my way. Just when I opened my mouth to ask why he hadn't left service to come looking for me, I felt a sweet sensation come over me, and God spoke to my heart.

Daughter, this was your journey to learn that I am with you no matter where you are, even until the end of the Earth.

About the Author

Florenza Denise Lee is an author, publisher, narrative coach, transformational speaker, radio talk show host, Master Storyteller, wife, mother, and advocate for our Nation's Veterans. Her Children's books focus on Social-Emotional Learning. Her dynamic characters immediately capture the readers' attention, and her lessons remain long after the book is closed. The tagline for her coaching business is, "…like having glasses for your mind." Florenza believes Christ uses simple principles to bring about profound truths. She applies this practical teaching method to guide her audience on a soul-searching journey to discover the power that lies within them. Florenza says her messages will stick with you like collard greens and cornbread.

She and her husband, CSM (Ret US Army) Trefus Lee, have been married for nearly 38 years and have recently relocated from Hampton, Virginia, to Chagrin Falls, Ohio. Their daughters, Jessica and Missy, call Las Vegas, Nevada, and Chagrin Falls, Ohio, home.

Please follow and engage virtually with Florenza via the following links.

Instagram: https://bit.ly/InstagramPagefld
Amazon Author: https://bit.ly/amazonauthorpagefdl
Kutafakari Bookstore: https://bit.ly/KutafakariBookstore
Facebook: https://www.facebook.com/Florenza.Denise.Lee/
Website: https://bit.ly/websitefdl
Mailing List https://bit.ly/StayInTheFlo
Pinterest http://bit.ly/PinterestFlo
BookBub: https://bit.ly/LeeFBookbub
GoodReads: https://bit.ly/LeeFGoodreads

The Merry Hearts Inspirational Series will warm your heart and touch your soul . . .

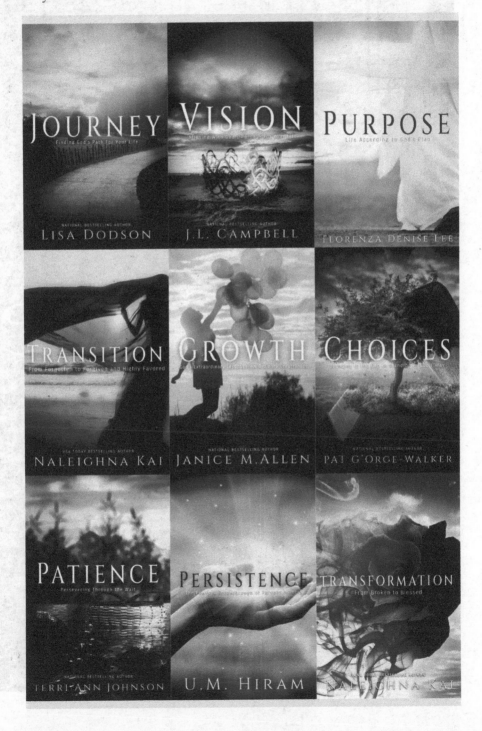

80 Days of Pleasure

AIKEN PONDER

QUEEN
OF
BELIZE

4

QUEENS OF THE CASTLE

AIKEN PONDER

Published titles by Florenza are:

Adventurous Olivia's Alphabet Quest
Adventurous Olivia's Calm Quest – A Book on Mindfulness
Amiri's Birthday Wish
Barry Bear's Very Best, Learning to Say No to Negative
Influences

Purpose: Life According to God's Plan

If…The Story of Faith Walker
Manny & Tutu
Mind Your Manners, Mia
There's No Place Like My Own Home
The Tail of Max the Mindless Dog, A Children's Book on
Mindfulness
Welcome Home, Daddy, Love, Lexi
When Life Gives Us Wind

Children's Books coming soon are:

Acornsville, Land of the Secret Seed Keepers
Adventurous Olivia's Numerical Quest
Adventurous Olivia's Garden Surprise
Brooklyn Beaver ALMOST Builds a Dam
Micah and Malik's Super Awesome Excellent Adventure
Oh, My Goodness, Look at this Big Mess
Two Bees in a Hive
Young Reader Chapter Books coming soon are:
Hoku to the Rescue
Two-Thirds is a Whole

For more information regarding Florenza's books or to
contact her to speak at your school or event, please visit
www.florenza.org.

www.florenza.org.

CPSIA information can be obtained
at www.ICGtesting.com
Printed in the USA
LVHW041056090721
692288LV00007B/337